The Next Step in
FOLK ART

The Next Step in
FOLK ART

Lea Davis

Kangaroo Press

Dedication
For Colin, in Heaven

Acknowledgments
I have been blessed with a loving husband and family who are always enthusiastic and willing to participate in my latest project. Nothing would have been possible without you. Thank you:
- Mike, Tim, Casey and Scott, always with love
- Philip, my wonderful husband
- Sue and Peter, my sister and brother-in-law
- Dot and Frank Charlton, my mum and dad

I would like to take this opportunity to thank some very special people who made the writing of this book so much easier:
- Carol and Graeme Scott (and of course, Lauren, Brett and Ashlee)
- Sally and Ian Luck, and Mr T and Mr W, two very well behaved bears who belong to Thomas and William Luck
- Pam Brown
- Sue Schirmer
- Jill Logue
- Karen Rowelle
- Joy Waters
- John Boyle
- Rowan Bavinton

I am indebted to Brice Dunkley for his wonderful photographs and for being so patient. Sally and Pam, thank you, from the bottom of my heart, for all your hard work.

I am also privileged to have Enid Hoessinger as my teacher and friend. Thank you, Enid, for everything you have shared with me.

To all my students, thank you for your enthusiasm and support. My life is richer for knowing you all.

© Lea Davis 1994

Reprinted 1995, 1997 and 1999
First published in 1994 by Kangaroo Press
an imprint of Simon & Schuster (Australia) Pty Limited
20 Barcoo Street, East Roseville NSW 2069
Printed in Hong Kong through Colorcraft

ISBN 0 86417 574 4

Contents

Introduction 7
Equipment and techniques 8
   Transferring a pattern 8
   Surface techniques 9
   Preparation procedures 10
   Glossary of brush loading techniques 10
Preparing a découpage picture 13
Roses step by step 14
Chrysanthemums step by step 16
Foliage 16

PROJECTS 18
Treasure chest 18
Poppy plaque 21
The plate 24
Writing slope 27
Lace box 31
Flower basket box 35
Memory box 38
Waiting stool 41
Picture frame 44
Pansy box 47
Photo album 50
Sally's cupboard 52
Michael's tray 56

PATTERNS 60

Suppliers 80
Index 80

INTRODUCTION

The patterns in this book use techniques which are extensions of the techniques used in my previous book, *Introduction to Folk Art*, also published by Kangaroo Press. The basic loading techniques become more involved, with sometimes three colours on the brush. (Please be sure to read and understand the instructions before beginning any piece.) The work is also more refined, with delicate little filler flowers and leaves. By now you should have had lots of practice with your strokes and I hope this book provides you with more inspiring pieces and techniques.

Most of the patterns can be adapted to fit other pieces: you should also feel free to change the colours.

Putting this book together was even more exciting than writing *Introduction to Folk Art*, as there was more scope to be creative.

I love the use of découpage in my work, as it allows great freedom and tremendous design possibilities. You can personalise your pieces by incorporating photographs or letters that are special to you. The découpage picture on the writing slope is an old postcard photograph of my great-grandmother, and the writing is from the backs of two of her postcards. If the card or photograph you want to use isn't the correct size for the design, you can have it enlarged or reduced when you get it colour photocopied.

If you haven't painted with a sable brush before, please consider purchasing one. These brushes have more bounce and spring than the acrylic fibre brushes and produce very fine lines. I have used a Rowney S40 throughout this book, but other teachers may have favourite sable brushes that they can recommend.

Good luck. Please keep me informed of your progress, or of any problems you may have by writing to me care of VADA, 369 Camberwell Rd, Camberwell, Victoria 3124.

EQUIPMENT AND TECHNIQUES

Brushes
For most of the work in this book I used a Rowney S40 Kolinsky Sable brush, size 4. Sable hairs are naturally thicker in the middle of the hair and because of this snap back to a point. By thinning the paint, and rolling such a brush to a point, you can make wonderfully thin lines, which is great if you are a lazy painter like me because you don't have to continually pick up and put down brushes. You may, however, prefer a liner brush such as Loew-Cornell's Jackie Shaw liner, size 1, or a Raphael Series 8220 liner. Either of these is great, but remember if you choose another brand to make sure it is a long liner brush; if it's not you will be continually reloading your brush with paint.

For basecoating my pieces I prefer to use a 25 mm (1") flat brush. They are rather expensive but give a beautiful finish. A cheaper alternative is a poly-sponge brush, which sells for around a couple of dollars, depending on the size.

Please take good care of your brushes. A build-up of paint near the ferrule can wreck a brush very quickly. Always remember to reshape brushes with soap after use.

Palette
I like to use a very thin dishwashing sponge to make a palette. These are available from supermarkets in packs of three. Cut one in half, wring it out in water (you don't need it wringing wet) and wrap it round with one layer of *greaseproof* paper. Place the paints onto the paper and they will stay moist for hours. When you have finished painting for the day you can lift the palette and place it in an airtight container where it will remain moist until next time you wish to paint. I like to use a Primo Palette, a small covered container which keeps paint moist for weeks. Cut the sponge and paper to fit in the container; the paints are placed on this. When you have finished painting for the day, mist lightly with water, and cover. It's great for taking to classes because it doesn't take up too much room.

Paper towel
Paper towelling is used to absorb water from the brushes. Place a few folded sheets next to your palette.

Sandpaper
You will need various grades of sandpaper for different stages of a project. I use #400 and #600 grit, wet-and-dry sandpaper. It is black in colour, and I use it *dry*. Use a sanding block, especially for larger surfaces, and sand with the grain.

Transferring a pattern

There are two ways of transferring a pattern. The first requires transfer or graphite paper from a craft store. These papers come in various colours, but you will only need a light colour for dark backgrounds and a dark colour for light backgrounds. After you have traced your chosen pattern and positioned it over the painting surface, slip the transfer paper (chalky side down) under your tracing. You can secure either or both with masking tape. Trace over your design, using a stylus, an empty ballpoint pen, or even a pencil. Don't press too hard or you may dent the surface. You will need to use an eraser to remove any lines which you haven't covered with your painting.

The second method uses ordinary blackboard chalk. Again you will need a variety of colours. Trace your chosen design onto *greaseproof* paper. Turn the design over and using an appropriate colour chalk for your base colour, rub the chalk over the back of the design. Rub the chalk into the paper with your finger and shake off the excess dust. Place the paper chalk side down onto your article and using a stylus or pencil as before, trace around the design.

Surface techniques

Sealing

I like to use a sealer mixed in with the base paint. I also give craftwood one coat of sealer before basecoating. Sand well, then mix the sealer and tube paint 1:1, and apply as you normally would. I use Jo Sonja's All-Purpose Sealer.

Antiquing

Antiquing gives the surface of a finished piece an aged appearance, imparting the same depth of tone to all the colours. There are two methods, oil-based and water-based. As I have used only the oil-based method in this book, I will give instructions for that method only. The instructions for both methods appear in full in my earlier book, Introduction to Folk Art, p.14 (Kangaroo Press, 1992).

Use this method in a well ventilated area. Wear disposable gloves and when the antiquing is finished, wet the rags you have been using and throw them in the rubbish bin. A few cases of spontaneous combustion have been reported following careless disposal of rags.

The oil-based method of antiquing usually removes graphite lines, but to be on the safe side remove them with an eraser anyway.

You will need patina oil made up of:
1 part refined linseed oil
4 parts gum or natural turpentine (*not* mineral)
Mix this together in a screwtop jar.
OR use Scottie's Antiquing Patina

You will also need *oil* paints, either Winsor and Newton or Rowney. I usually use Burnt Umber, but consider also Raw Umber, Burnt Sienna, Black, Indigo Blue, Prussian Blue and Raw Sienna.
Squares of lint-free cotton cloth

A few hints before you start:
1. Work one surface at a time. Oil paints take much longer to dry than acrylics and it's woefully easy to leave fingermarks on a surface which has been newly antiqued.
2. Any slopovers, e.g. on a side that you haven't antiqued yet, underneath or inside, should be wiped off quickly.
3. If you don't like the colour or the way it looks you can remove nearly all of it by moistening a clean cloth with the patina oil mix and wiping it off. Don't leave it to dry before you decide you don't like it—it must be removed fairly quickly.

Procedure
Moisten a small area of a clean cotton square with the patina oil mix. Wipe this over the area to be antiqued, making sure the entire surface has been covered and there are no puddles or drips. Now, on the same area of cloth that you applied the patina with, pick up a small amount of tube oil paint. Stroke this onto the surface with smooth even strokes until the whole area has been covered. Take a clean cotton rag and smooth out the antiquing to the desired depth. It looks more effective when the edges are darker than the middle. Make sure the antiquing gets into all the joints and crevices. You may need an old brush to do this. If you would like certain areas lighter, remove the antiquing with a cotton bud dipped in the patina oil mix. Smooth out the area afterwards. Try and bring contrast into the finish. *Do not use water-based varnishes over oil-based antiquing.*

Varnishing

There are many types of varnishes available. Choose one that is appropriate to the finish you require. The water-based varnishes are so easy to use and dry so quickly that you can put on a couple of coats in quick succession. The solvent-based products take longer to dry, especially in winter. Jo Sonja's solvent-based varnish is excellent, as is Feast-Watson's oil-based polyurethane varnish.

Apply both with a 25 mm (1″) flat brush, sanding lightly between coats. Wipe off any sanding dust with a damp cloth, making certain the surface is thoroughly dry before proceeding.

Preparation procedures

Wood

Make sure the surface you have chosen to paint has been sealed and sanded. Use a 25 mm (1") flat brush or a poly-sponge brush to coat the surface with the base colour. Sand lightly and recoat. Depending on the colour chosen you may need several successive coats. Usually the lighter colours need more coats. Allow to dry thoroughly once you have sufficient coverage. Using old worn sandpaper, lightly sand the surface one final time. You are now ready to apply your pattern.

Metal

Make certain the surface is in sound condition before you start painting. On new metal, wash the surface with a vinegar and water solution and then apply a primer. I like to use a black etch primer, which dries very quickly (see Suppliers, page 80). Now apply the base colour, with Jo Sonja All-Purpose Sealer added to it, with either a flat brush or a poly-sponge brush.

Please refer to my book *Introduction to Folk Art* for thorough discussion of all these areas (Kangaroo Press, 1992).

Glossary of brush loading techniques

The book assumes prior knowledge of the basic techniques of folk art painting, as covered in *Introduction to Folk Art*. However, the techniques marked ★ are more advanced and will require practice.

'To the surface'/'to the ceiling'
The instructions will sometimes ask you to hold the brush in a particular way or to apply the colour in a particular direction. This will usually be 'to the surface' or 'to the ceiling'. Do not get this confused with 'top' or 'bottom', which refers to the top or bottom of your piece (or page if you are practising).

Basic loading
Usually referred to in the instructions as a 'load'. Dress the brush in a single colour, making sure the brush is not bloated with paint. In most cases the hairs of the brush should still be visible through the paint.

Knife edge and knife stroke
While loading the brush, flatten the hairs gently by sweeping through the paint a few times. You will notice you now have a flat side and a narrow side. The flat side is referred to as just that, the 'flat', and the narrow side is the 'chisel' or 'knife' edge. By turning the brush onto the knife edge and using very light pressure you will be able to make fine lines by pulling the brush towards you. The knife edge is used frequently to paint the veins on leaves and stems, and wherever you need fine straight or slightly curved lines. To paint very thin curly lines you must thin the paint down with water, roll the brush to a point and keep it upright. If the lines are too wide and watery, then the paint is too thin.

Wash
This is really a lot like watercolour painting. Thin the paint with water, but test the depth of colour on a scrap piece of paper before you start painting. Keep some paper towel handy. After you have mixed the correct colour and consistency of paint, touch the loaded brush to the paper towel before you start painting. This will help prevent puddles on your piece. Remember it is much better to have the paint fairly transparent. You can always recoat a washed area, but you will get into all sorts of trouble if the paint is too dark and you try to remove it.

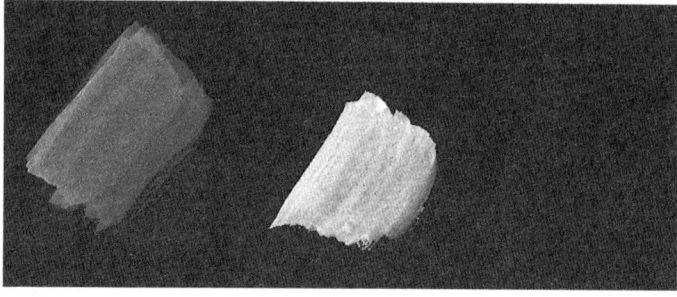

Left: *Correct wash technique resulting in transparent colour; on the right, too much paint results in solid or opaque colour*

Stipple
Take a colour, or even two, and dab the brush up and down lightly in the area to be covered. Usually used as the centres for daisies or blossoms. It leaves a mottled effect rather than a solid colour.

The colours used here are Antique Gold Deep, to load the brush, and White Wash to tip it

★ **Sweep**
After loading the brush in the main colour, pull out a small amount of the second colour from the puddle of paint and sweep or wipe the hairs of the brush through this. You will not be loading the brush, but rather pushing the other colour onto the hairs. Do not aim for a great deal of paint.

The instructions will usually ask you to sweep through Yellow Light or Antique Gold, but sometimes other colours are used. When using this method of loading, the Antique Gold or Yellow Light will act as a buffer between the first load and the last colour, which is usually white. As an example, your brush could have the following colours in this order: Load in Oxblood, sweep through Yellow Light, and sideload in Snow White. In this case the Yellow Light acts as a buffer between the orange (Oxblood) and the white. Without the Yellow Light the colour would be a bland apricot.

★ **Side load**
After loading the brush in colour, push the brush horizontally into the puddle of white paint and pull it out towards you. It helps to have a strip of paint rather than a puddle. You should have white paint only on one side of the brush.

★ **Tipping**
After loading the brush in one colour, tip the end of one side of the brush onto the puddle of the second colour. You will now have a small amount of paint on the end of the brush which is ideal for painting small things. This is the same as side loading except on a smaller scale.

★ **Fan-out centre**
Some of the designs in this book use the fan-out centre, an advanced technique. As you can see from the diagram, there are three colours visible. First, load the brush in the main colour. I used Burnt Sienna for the example (made from Napthol Red Light and Antique Green). On the tip of the brush, on one side only, take on a small amount of Antique Gold. On the opposite side, near the ferrule or metal ring, take on a dot of Black.

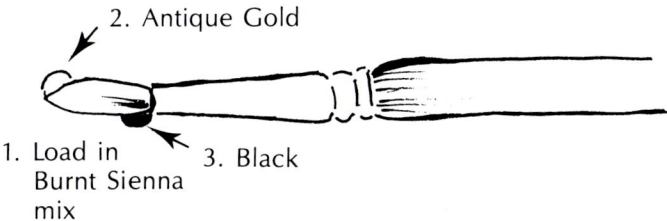

Correct brush loading technique

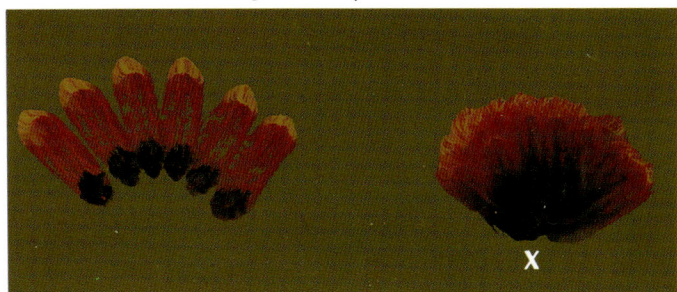

Fan-out technique—pivot the brush from X

Now lay the brush down in the pattern area with the black to the surface and fan out the strokes in an arch. Make sure you don't go back over what you have done as you can blend the colours together and end up with mud.

Try to keep the ferrule almost in the one spot and pivot from there. If you feel the paint is a little dry, then touch the tip into a tiny drop of water before you begin. If you aren't happy with what you have done, then let it dry before you try again.

The instructions give you the colours in the order they are to be used. For example, if the instructions say, 'Fan out the centre using Oxblood, Yellow Light and Black', you would load the brush in Oxblood, on the tip of the brush on one side take on Yellow Light, and on the opposite side near the ferrule take on a spot of Black.

★ **Pull-in**
Using the side loading technique pick up a load of paint and lay it down on the paper following the shape of the petal. The colour will most probably be white, but could be anything. Wipe off the excess paint on some paper towel, and wipe the brush in the flower colour, making sure the hairs on the brush flatten out. Push the flattened tip under the ridge of paint and pull the colour down to the middle of the flower in the appropriate direction. Wipe off excess paint, reload in the flower colour and repeat until you have moved along the ridge of paint. Repeat for the rest of the flower, working one petal at a time.

There are a few things to remember about the pull-in:
1. Aim for a thick ridge of paint around the edge of the petals.
2. Wipe off the excess paint from the brush. Try to keep the brush out of the water unless you find it dragging across your work.
3. Spread the hairs on the brush so they fan out.
4. Always pull the strokes in the flower colour, in the direction of growth.

★ Dry brushing

Used to place a hint of colour in a given area. Load the brush by sweeping the hairs through the paint. The paint brush should be flattened—if it isn't then flatten it. Now, using the tips of the hairs, whisk the paint over the area to be covered. You should have only the barest hint of colour which you can reinforce by repeating what you have done. It is far better to start off lightly than to end up with too much paint.

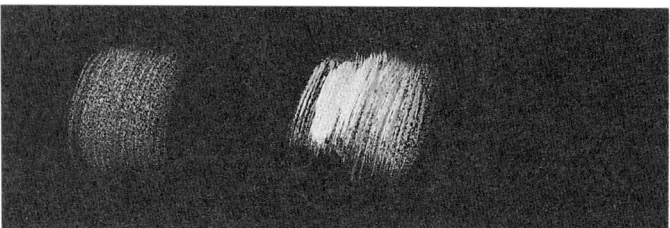

Left: Correct dry brushing technique— little paint, light pressure; on the right, incorrect technique—too much paint, too much pressure

When dry brushing fan out the hairs on the brush before applying the paint

PREPARING A DÉCOUPAGE PICTURE

Découpage pictures are used on the writing slope (page 27) and the photo album (page 50).

Merope Mills shared this method of preparing découpage pictures with us on a recent visit to Melbourne. There are a few other ways to approach this technique, but this one leaves you with the original picture.

Firstly you will need a picture the size the pattern calls for. If you cannot find one then consider having one that you like enlarged by colour photocopying. Four postcards (the old-fashioned kind) or postcard sized pictures will fit on one A4 sheet of paper. Tack them in place. As most copying places charge per sheet this could save you money. Be sure the colour photocopy you are paying for is *not* on photographic paper. Some photographic developers do beautiful colour copying onto thick photographic paper which is not suitable for what we are doing here.

Method
You will need: Jo Sonja All-Purpose Sealer, disposable gloves.

Place the picture to be découpaged face up on a piece of plastic. Put on the disposable gloves and, using your finger, apply a thin layer of sealer horizontally across the picture, starting at the top and working to the bottom. Be sure to start off the edge of the picture (i.e. on the plastic surround) to avoid a build-up of sealer on the edges. Lift the picture carefully and place it to dry on a clean sheet of plastic (otherwise it will stick to the first sheet of plastic). When this first coat is dry apply the sealer vertically, again smoothing the sealer out thinly. You will need to build up six coats of sealer, alternating the direction each time. Make sure each coat is dry before applying the next. It's also a good idea to keep the picture out of the way of cats, kids and breezes.

When dry, trim the picture to the correct size for the pattern. Using a container large enough to allow the picture to lie flat, fill with enough hot (not boiling) water to float the picture. Leave overnight. The sealer will go milky (but don't worry, it will dry clear). Next day, lay the picture, sealer side down, on plastic on a smooth surface and start rubbing off the paper very gently. You will find it very easy to do this. Keep going until all the paper has been removed and you are left with a thin membrane of sealer with the picture impregnated in it. Great! If you are in doubt as to whether you have removed all the paper, leave it to dry for a little while. If you still see a lot of white, keep going. You will need to remoisten the area first though.

Let the picture dry on a soft cloth. That's it!

ROSES STEP BY STEP

Before beginning this rose please revise the Glossary of Brush Loading Techniques on page 10.

Palette (Jo Sonja colours)
Burnt Sienna (Antique Green + Napthol Red Light)
Antique Gold
Black
White

1. Refer to the Glossary for the fan-out centres and using Burnt Sienna (made from Antique Green and Napthol Red Light), Antique Gold and Black, place the centre in. You will go over the pattern lines, so have the original pattern in front of you to follow.
   Sideload the white and, following the pattern lines for the back petals, push off the white. Wipe the brush and sweep through Burnt Sienna, then Antique Gold. The brush hairs should be flattened out. Now with the Antique Gold side facing the surface, push under the ridge and pull the white down. You will only need to use small strokes. Wipe the brush—do not wash.
2. Sideload again in white and following the pattern lay down the white. Wipe the brush, sweep through Burnt Sienna and Antique Gold, pulling the strokes down towards the middle of the flower.
3. Repeat the same steps for this petal, making certain to link up with the back petals. Use only light pressure and keep up on the tip of the brush when starting off. You may need to reload the white to complete the ridge.
4. Repeat the same steps, but don't link up the petal at the back.
5. Repeat again, but this time sweep through the white as well after sweeping through the Burnt Sienna and Antique Gold. By increasing the white on the front petal we are actually bringing the petal forward and giving the appearance of roundness.
6. Side petals. These are painted in exactly the same way as the petals on the body of the rose. The two back petals are painted first—remember to keep an eye on the direction of your strokes. Always try and pull the strokes towards you, so turn your work around when necessary. Paint the remaining petals.

   The turnback is painted separately, after the petals are all painted. Load the brush in the main flower colour and tip the brush in white. Hold the flower colour to the bottom of the petal and push the white up. Use gentle pressure.

   Tiny white lines are placed in the centre. You may like to have little dots, in which case tip the brush in Antique Gold, then white, and softly tap these in. Don't overdo these.

CHRYSANTHEMUMS STEP BY STEP

Chrysanthemums are easy flowers to paint once you know how. (Instructions for a slightly simpler sort appear in the Flower Basket Project on page 35.)

Palette (DecoArt colours)
Oxblood
Antique Gold Deep
Ebony Black
Snow White

1. Fan-out the centre (see page 11). I have used Oxblood, Antique Gold Deep and Ebony Black. Wash the brush.
2. Load in Oxblood, sweep through Antique Gold Deep, then sweep through Snow White. Starting at the back of the flower, and with the white held to the surface, paint the two back petals on either side of the body of the flower.
3. Sweep through the white, only once, and repeat what you have done. It is important that stroke no. 3 is in front of stroke no. 1.
4. Increase the white and repeat.
5. This is the last stroke. Increase the white again and pull the stroke over those on either side. You should have increased the white on petals numbered 1, 3, 5 and 7.

The frilly skirt Working one petal at a time, push out the edge with Snow White. Pull the white down with the brush loaded in Oxblood and swept in Antique Gold Deep.

The comma stroke skirt Use the same colours as before, but instead of sweeping through the Snow White, sideload it. Hold the white to the outside, and pull the strokes to the centre bottom of the flower. The stamens are tiny strokes of white.

FOLIAGE

The large leaves behind many of the designs are painted first. They are blocked in with no ridges and you may need two coats. Use the colours given in the instructions for particular projects. Mix enough paint for the project and store it somewhere on your wet palette, as you will need this colour again. Don't stop at the edge of the flower pattern when painting in a leaf, but continue over the lines a little. When you come to paint the flower it might not quite fill the area, and you could be left with a gap between the edge of the flower and the end of the leaf.

Paint all the stems with the dark leaf mix, but sweep through a little Antique Gold first, making a knife edge and pulling the stems with this.

On light coloured backgrounds (for example, Sally's Cupboard, page 52) you will need to wash some leaf shapes in behind the main dark foliage. Do this first, before the pattern is drawn. Lightly mark the perimeter of the design with chalk and using the dark foliage mix thinned with water paint in leaf shapes randomly. This is good practice, but make sure all the stems connect in the middle. The idea is to fill up the area and add bulk, but don't just block in the area as this is too uninteresting. Wash leaves do not have knife strokes or other embellishments.

When the flowers have been painted go back to the foliage and, using the knife edge of the brush, place delicate knife strokes on the leaves for the veins. Comma strokes and filler leaves can be added now if you feel there is an empty area.

1

2

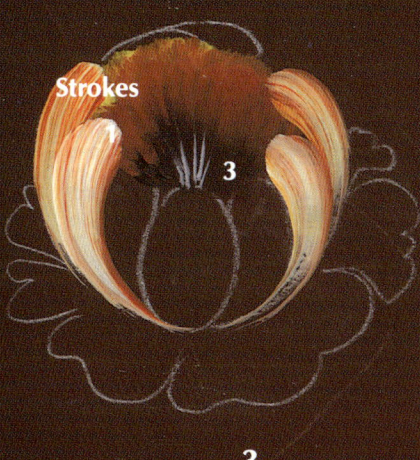

Strokes

3

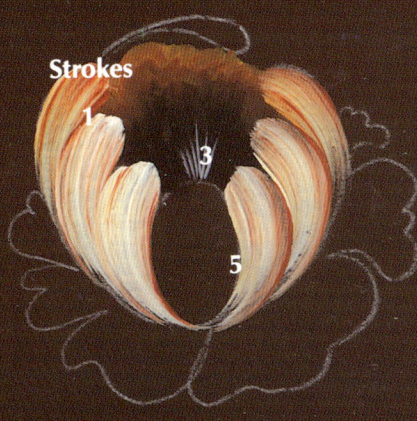

Strokes

4

5

ALTERNATIVE SKIRTS

Frilly skirt—push out the edges—pull the white down

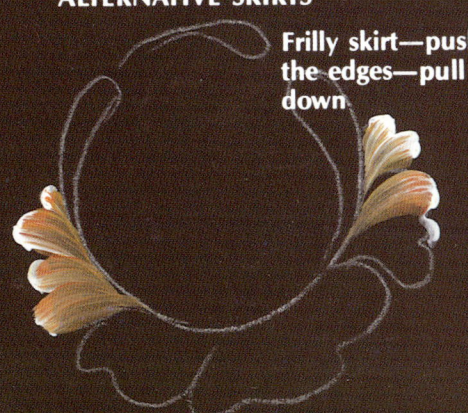

Comma stroke skirt

Turn-back

PROJECTS

Treasure chest
Pattern on page 60

Palette (DecoArt colours)
Cadmium Orange
Snow White
Antique Green
Ebony Black
Glorious Gold
Deep Burgundy
Blue Violet
Red Violet
Williamsburg Blue
Brilliant Red
Cadmium Yellow
Sealer
Jo Sonja Clear Glazing Medium

Because this little chest is made of craftwood, seal the surface first with one coat of sealer. Basecoat with Snow White. You will need at least six coats. Dry. Because white gets so dirty, I gave my piece one coat of Jo Sonja Clear Glazing Medium.

The pattern, which was inspired by pieces of eighteenth century Meissen porcelain, is applied randomly over the surface of the piece. The only rule I have is to keep the stems pointing towards the bottom, but you can please yourself on that account. The numbers beside the flowers on the colour work-up refer to the instructions below. All foliage is painted in the same mix of Antique Green + Ebony Black.

1. Forget-me-nots
Mix: 1 part Blue Violet
½ part Williamsburg Blue
⅛ part Red Violet
Just a touch of Brilliant Red

Start at the top of the tiny bud and work down. Wipe through a small amount of Snow White for the front petals of each flower. Hold the white to the surface. Centres are Cadmium Yellow dots.

2. Rose Paint a Deep Burgundy circle. Sideload in Snow White and paint in the two back petals, then the two comma strokes on the body of the rose. You may need to replace the Snow White on the tip of the brush to complete the last three remaining petals. Place the ones on either side first, then the one underneath.

3. Bluebells Paint the back petals first in Cadmium Yellow. Load the brush in Blue Violet and paint S strokes for either side of the bell. Sweep through Snow White and, holding the white to the surface, place the front petal in.

4. Orange daisies Paint the back petals in Oxblood. Wipe through Yellow Light, hold this to the surface, and paint the remainder. For the smaller side flower, paint the back petals in the Oxblood/Yellow Light combination, then the other petals in Oxblood. Centres are Yellow Light. Ebony Black stamens.

19

5. Paint the back petals with a little watery Deep Burgundy. The front petals are Deep Burgundy straight. The centres are Antique Green sideloaded in Yellow Light.

6. Place the back petals in with Oxblood + Yellow Light. Sweep through Yellow Light for the front petals. The centres are tiny black dots.

7. Paint the back petals Cadmium Orange, then sweep through Yellow Light for the front petals. Calyxes are in the leaf mix of Antique Green + Ebony Black.

8. Mix Yellow Light + Antique Gold for the back petals, then sideload in Antique Green for the front ones. Leave the tiniest ones on the tip free of the Antique Green.

Insects and birds These are all outlined in Ebony Black with very thin paint. Decorate them as desired, with the colours from your palette. Be sure to use delicate washes of colour.

Gold foliage This is placed in randomly with Glorious Gold. Keep small.

Dot flowers Painted in Deep Burgundy with Blue Violet centres.

Linework The line around the edge is painted with thinned Glorious Gold. Stop and start the line every now and then to get variation. Don't aim for perfection.

Varnish with three coats of varnish.

Poppy plaque
Pattern on pages 62–63

Palette (Jo Sonja colours)
Antique Green
Carbon Black
Napthol Red Light
Napthol Crimson
Antique Gold
Raw Sienna
Burnt Umber
Titanium White
Warm White

Basecoat your chosen piece with Antique Green. Sand between coats and trace on the leaves from the pattern only.

Leaves Make a dark leaf mix by mixing Antique Green with Carbon Black. Sideload the brush in straight Antique Green and pull the strokes in towards the centre vein. Poppy leaves twist and turn, so try and have some edges lighter and others darker. Using the dark mix, wash in some distant foliage. It is easier to freehand this in. Trace on the rest of the design. Remember to pull all the stems under the poppies.

Poppies The petals are numbered on both the poppies. We will work through the red one.

Sideload in Napthol Red Light and lay down the colour following the pattern lines. Wipe the brush and sweep in Napthol Crimson, then once in Burnt Umber, flattening the brush as you go. Gently push the brush under the ridge of Napthol Red Light and pull the colour down. If you need to replenish the colour, then sweep only through the Napthol Crimson. Repeat for the rest of the petals. The direction of your strokes is most important, so please take note of where the strokes are going.

Before you paint petals 6 and 7, you may find it easier to paint the centre. Block in the area with Burnt Umber then place small vertical lines in Antique Gold.

See how the turnback stands out against the other petals

You will notice on the colour work-up that I have indicated a turnback on the front petal. See how it stands out against the other petals. I have underpainted that small area with Titanium White and then let it dry. Sideload in Napthol Red Light and finish the petal as normal. Because the Napthol Red Light is fairly transparent, the white underpainting shows through, making the petal really vibrant.

The white poppy is completed the same way. The colours are Titanium White for the sideload, Warm White for the main colour and a *little* Raw Sienna for the shade colour. The centre is based in the dark green leaf mix, but while this is still wet place curved lines in Antique Gold. The dots are Antique Gold, Antique Green + Black and Warm White.

The closed red poppy uses the same colours as the open red poppy except that the sideload for the edge of the petals is Warm White.

The poppy bud Load the brush in Napthol Scarlet, then sweep through the Antique Gold and lift the white (either white will do). Place the white to the surface and apply pressure—you should have a blob. Now, using the dark leaf mix, sweep through a little Antique Gold and place two comma strokes on either side of the blob, and just overlapping the edges. The stem is the same dark leaf mix.

Daisies Load the brush in Warm White and sweep through a little Antique Green. Hold the Antique Green to the surface as you paint the petals. The centres are Antique Gold, with a little Burnt Sienna (made from Napthol Red Light + Antique Green) worked into the bottom of the centre area. A little Titanium White can be used as a highlight on the opposite side to the Burnt Sienna. The stems and calyxes are the same dark mix used on the leaves, but sweep through a little Antique Gold.

Dandelion seeds Thin Titanium White with water and place in tiny little strokes, about five in each seed, randomly over the design area. They should join up at the bottom. Sideload the tip of the brush in Antique Gold and with very gentle pressure, drop in the seed.

Antique lightly with Burnt Sienna and finish with the appropriate varnish.

The plate
Pattern on page 61

Palette (DecoArt colours)
Fleshtone
Buttermilk
Ebony Black
Antique Green
Brilliant Red
Antique Gold Deep
True Blue

Seal the surface of the plate with straight sealer. Sand well. Apply a Buttermilk basecoat with a large brush, aiming for a good finish with no ridges. Dry, and sand lightly.

Take some newspaper and tear it into strips about 12 cm (5″) long by 7 cm (3″) wide (you will only need a few unless you are really messy). Have these prepared before you start working. Roll the strips up loosely and squash them into the palm of your hand. You will be making little balls with

25

a flat side, and you will be using these to work the paint.

Apply the Fleshtone with a large brush to half the rim. Now quickly push the crumpled paper ball in a twisting motion over the wet paint. You will notice that you are picking up the Fleshtone exposing the Buttermilk basecoat underneath. By working the paint in sections you can control the finish without getting flustered. Finish the rim and the centre of the plate in the same way. When working the centre, keep the area underneath the pattern free of ridges. I lightly chalked a line around the edge of the pattern area before I applied the paint. Dry and apply the pattern.

Leaves and stems Block in with a dark mix of Antique Green and Ebony Black. Where one leaf overlaps the other, sideload the brush in a small amount of Antique Gold Deep and blend it down the side of the top leaf. The knife strokes are the dark leaf mix swept through Antique Gold Deep.

Rose Refer to the colour work-up on page 14. Fan-out the centre using Antique Green + Brilliant Red to make a warm brown (Burnt Sienna mix), Antique Gold Deep and Ebony Black. Load the brush in the Burnt Sienna mix, sweep through Antique Gold Deep, and use this to pull the Snow White edge down.

Tulips Refer to the colour work-up. The colours are the same as for the rose—Burnt Sienna mix, then sweep through Antique Gold Deep, sideload in Snow White. Lay the white down along the pattern lines for the back two petals, then load the brush in the above colours and pull the white down. Repeat for the two side petals, then lastly the middle one.

Daisies Mix True Blue + Ebony Black to get a muted blue. Push out the edges in Snow White and pull the strokes for each petal down in the blue mix.

Antique with Burnt Umber oil paint using the method on page 9. When the antiquing is dry (in about 7–10 days, depending on the weather) take 0000 or 000 size steel wool and a good quality paste wax and buff the surface. You will see the ridges of Fleshtone stand out where the antiquing has been rubbed off. There is no need to varnish as the wax protects the surface.

Writing slope
Pattern on pages 64–65

For this project you will need three postcards. See the instructions for preparing a découpage picture on page 13 before beginning.

You will need to apply the postcards before you begin painting. It doesn't matter which one you choose to stick down first, but as yours won't be the same as those here, take the overall effect into account. I have used one vertical picture for the side, and two written cards for the bottom. Remember this piece has a lot of work on it, so that using more than one picture or photograph may make it too busy. (Of course this will depend on what you have chosen.) It is important to use a pine article to work on as we want the wonderful grain of the wood to show through. When Nature has created something as wonderful as wood, why cover it up? As wood ages it mellows, and you will have with this piece a most wonderful addition to your family heirlooms.

Palette (Jo Sonja colours)
Teal Green
Smoked Pearl
Napthol Red Light
Antique Green
Diox Purple
French Blue
Burnt Umber
Raw Sienna
Plum Pink
Carbon Black
Titanium White
Antique Gold
Ultramarine Blue

Position the découpaged cards (or pictures) on the surface according to the confines of the pattern. Place small chalk marks around the edges so you will know where they belong when you remove them to stick them down. Apply Jo Sonja All-Purpose Sealer on their backs and carefully stick them down. Try to keep the wood around the pictures free of sealer as it will seal the surface and the washes that are applied later will not be accepted into the grain. It will also leave a noticeable bald spot. Keep a damp rag nearby and wipe the area surrounding the cards frequently. Let dry overnight. Never use a hairdryer on the découpaged pictures as they will bubble and lift.

Using a large flat brush and watery Smoked Pearl apply one coat to the entire surface, omitting the découpage area. Now mix Teal Green + Smoked Pearl with a little water and apply this mix in a grid or brick pattern underneath the design area. It doesn't have to be even or straight. All you are doing is adding depth behind the design. Don't go outside the pattern area though. When you are satisfied, let dry, then sand lightly. Apply one coat of Clear Glazing Medium. Dry. Trace on the design remembering to use light pressure.

Leaves The darkest leaves, usually the rose leaves, are Antique Green + Carbon Black and have knife strokes on the top. With any of the leaves you could try any of the following colour mixes. Try and keep the same colour mix to each family of flowers, although with some areas of the pattern it's a little hard to tell who belongs to what! The choices are:
  Antique Green + Carbon Black
  Antique Green + Teal Green + touch Carbon Black
  Teal Green
  Teal Green + Titanium White
All the tiny filler strokes and commas are painted in any of the above mixes as well. Do remember to water any of the choices down and paint in some wash leaves. The knife strokes are made with the leaf mix you have chosen swept through Antique Gold.

Pink blossoms (on the vine up the left side) The vine is painted first with Antique Green + Carbon Black. Sweet through a little Antique Gold, and hold this to the surface. The vine is wavy with little tendrils sprouting off it. Don't be too fussy, as there is a lot of work to go on top. The blossoms are painted in Plum Pink. Work one petal at a time, pushing out the edge in Titanium White. Pull down with Plum Pink. They have tiny Burnt Umber stamens and Titanium White dots.

Roses All the roses are painted in the same mix, but try and vary the amount of white you pull down so they don't all look the same. The edge is again pushed out in Titanium White. Mix Napthol Red Light + Antique Green + Titanium White, to get a soft pink. Add more white to a little of this to give you another tint of the main mix. Try and keep the back or underneath petals darker than the fronts of the roses. The dying calyx is painted in the Antique Green + Carbon Black mix. Load the brush in this, sweep through a little Antique Gold, hold this to the surface, and paint the strokes. The stamens are Burnt Umber, then Burnt Umber + White. Thin the paint and keep up on the tip of the brush. Dots are Titanium White, Antique Gold and Burnt Umber.

White wood violets The back petals are painted in a soft mix of Teal Green + Titanium White. The front ones are straight Titanium White. Place a tiny Yellow Oxide dot in the centre.

Forget-me-nots Make a mix from the following:
  1 part Ultramarine Blue
  ½ part French Blue
  ⅛ part Diox Purple
  Just a touch of Napthol Red Light

Load the brush in this, sideload in Titanium White and place the petals in groups of five. The flowers have Antique Gold centres.

Purple violets Using the same mix as for the Forget-me-nots, place the back petals in. Sweep through Titanium White for the front petals. Yellow Oxide dots for the centres.

Peach blossom (near the bird's nest) Block in the shape with Warm White. Wash over the ends of the petals with the same soft pink mix that you used for the roses. Stamens are Titanium White, with Yellow Oxide dots.

Bird Base the breast area with Warm White. The wings, back and head are Burnt Umber. You will probably need two coats on both. When dry, mix a little Carbon Black with

Burnt Umber and outline the feathers. Soften the line between the white and brown with tiny little comma strokes. The beak is Carbon Black + Warm White. The feet and legs are Burnt Umber. The eye is Carbon Black with a Titanium White highlight.

Branch Load the brush in Burnt Umber then sweep through Antique Gold. Hold the gold to the surface and place in the line. Don't make it even. Paint tiny curved lines down the branch to resemble the bark. Add a little Warm White to the brush and place in some highlights.

Nest Wash in underneath the nest area with Burnt Umber, but don't take it to the very edge of the nest pattern. Using Burnt Umber make numerous lines to fill in the area. Add a little Warm White and work this in also. I added a few strokes of Yellow Oxide, but keep them small. You will find that you need to work this for a while. The eggs are Burnt Umber + Warm White. Dry brush Warm White highlights on to the tops of the shells. Add watery dots of Burnt Umber.

Butterflies The pale yellow butterfly is based in Warm White. Wash Yellow Oxide onto the two front wings. The body and antennae are Burnt Umber. The brown butterfly again uses Yellow Oxide for the back wings (only the tips are visible), then Yellow Oxide + Warm White for the front wings. The body and linework are Burnt Umber. The blue dots are Ultramarine + Burnt Umber. On top of this is a Yellow Oxide + Warm White dot.

When everything is dry, antique very lightly with Burnt Umber. Finish with three coats of an appropriate varnish.

Lace box
Pattern on pages 66–67

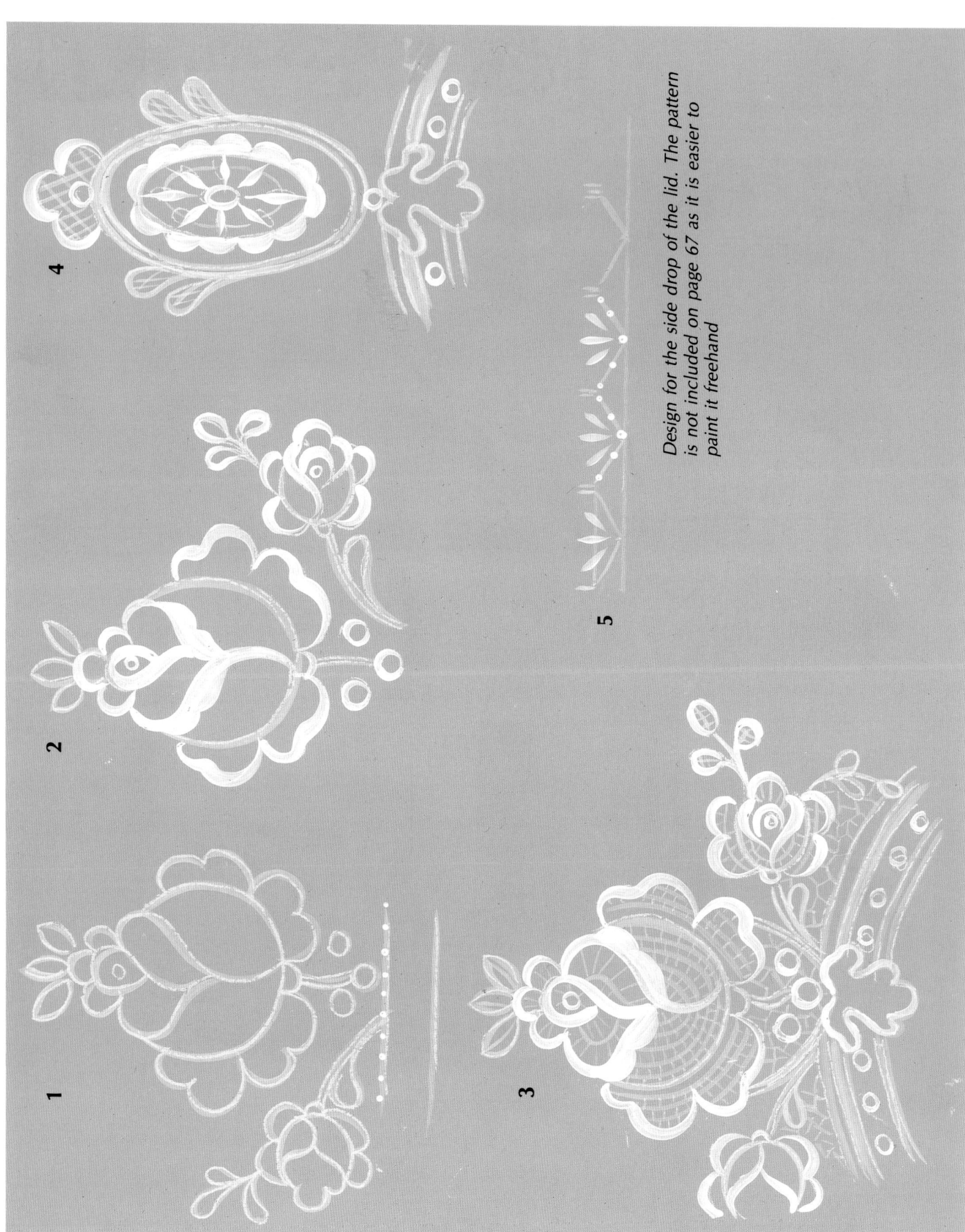

This piece is very easy to paint, although quite time consuming. It would make a lovely Bride Box.

Palette (Jo Sonja colours)
Opal
Titanium White

Stencil (optional)
Plaid Enterprises Stencil No. 28803, 'Personally Yours' 4 cm (1½")

Basecoat the box in Opal. Trace the pattern on with white transfer paper and a *very* fine stylus. Don't press so hard you dent the surface.

The first step involves thinning the Titanium White with sufficient water to enable you to paint lovely thin lines. You may like to use a liner brush. Thick watery lines may mean you have the paint too thin. It helps to touch the tip of the brush lightly onto paper towel after loading and before going onto your piece.

Draw around all the main lines of the pattern once. See step 1 in the picture.

In step 2 you can see which lines I have recoated with thick paint. Try and give them lots of texture.

Step 3 shows all the tiny embroidery lines. Keep up on the very tip of the brush.

Step 4 shows the large medallion for the lid pattern. There are four of these on the lid. The pattern shows only two of them, so you will need to adjust it.

Step 5 is the design for the lid drop.

Dots are best left until last.

I painted my initials in the centre of the lid using a stencil. The one I chose has large 4 cm (1½") letters. Trace around their edges with a sharp white chalk pencil and paint in thinned white. Recoat as many times as necessary. I placed tiny dots through the middle of each initial.

This design is not prescriptive—you can interpret it however you wish.

After all the painting has been done, check to see you haven't forgotten anything. Antique *lightly* with Burnt Umber and leave to dry. When completely dry, use 000 or 0000 steel wool to lightly buff the surface. You will see the thick white ridges pop up.

Finish by varnishing or waxing as you prefer.

If you used your liner brush for this you are now an expert!

Flower basket box
Pattern on pages 70–71

Palette (DecoArt colours)
Black Forest Green
Raw Sienna
Burnt Umber
Yellow Light
Oxblood
Antique Green
Antique Gold Deep
Snow White
Brilliant Red
Ebony (Lamp) Black
sea sponge
plastic wrap
Retarder

Using Black Forest Green basecoat the surface. You will probably need three coats. If possible leave overnight to cure.

Moisten the surface with watery Black Forest Green and apply watery Antique Gold with a sea sponge. Tear off a large sheet of plastic wrap and drop this onto the surface. Using your fingers, move the plastic gently to create gathers and pleats in it. Carefully lift off the plastic and let the surface dry.

Basket Apply the basket pattern using the chalk method on page 8. Moisten the area with Retarder. Do not use too much—the surface should appear satiny, not shiny wet. Using Antique Gold Deep apply the colour evenly over the basket area (but not to the handle yet). Wipe the brush in the Snow White and, starting at the left of the pattern, walk the colour across to the other side. Do not reload and do not stop halfway across—keep going even though it looks as though you have run out of paint. Once across the other side you can go back, but you mustn't stop halfway through.

Now, clean the brush and make a warm red-brown by mixing Brilliant Red + Antique Green; repeat the procedure but start at the right-hand side.

Mix a little Burnt Umber into the Red/Green mix to darken, and place in the lines on the basket. There are also fine horizontal lines on the basket, on the light side only. Keep them muted.

The back area of the handle is painted with Burnt Umber + Antique Gold. Use S strokes to fill in the area. The front of the handle is Antique Gold Deep wiped in Snow White, again using S strokes. Let dry and apply the rest of the pattern. You can omit the tiny flowers if you like and freehand them in later.

Leaves Mix Black Forest Green + Ebony Black. This mix should be very dark, but not black. Base in all the leaves in solid colour. The knife strokes are the same dark leaf mix, swept through Antique Gold Deep.

Tulip leaves Dark mix + sideload of Antique Gold Deep.

Stems and comma strokes Dark leaf mix, then sweep through Antique Gold Deep.

Cup roses See colour work-up on page 14. Push out the edge of each petal with Snow White. Wipe the brush first in Oxblood then in Antique Gold Deep and pull the white down.

Ball flowers Softly base in with watery Black Forest Green, then darken the outside edge with a little Ebony Black. Wash the brush and, while the surface is still wet, pick up a little Snow White and quickly place in irregular shaped petals in clusters of five. Keep the strongest colour in the centre. Dots in the middle are Snow White.

Large yellow daisies Push out the edges of the daisy petals with Snow White, making sure to work only one petal at a time. Wipe the brush and sweep into Antique Gold Deep (this is for the back daisy). Pull the White into the centre. Repeat for the front daisy but, after sweeping through the Antique Gold Deep, sweep again through the Yellow Light, and then pull the white down. The centres are Antique Gold Deep, with Oxblood dabbled into the shaded area and Snow White as the highlight.

White daisies Load the brush in Snow White, then sweep through the Antique Green and place in the back petals. As you work to the front of the flower wipe back in the white on the white side to increase the colour. The centres are Yellow Light dabbled in.

Yellow frilly chrysanthemum Fan-out the centre using Oxblood, Antique Gold Deep and Ebony Black. Wash the brush, load in Yellow Light and sweep in Snow White. Starting at the back of the flower, and with the Snow White held to the surface, paint the two back petals on either side of the body, then sweep into Snow White again and paint the next two. Increase the white again for the next two and paint those. Lastly sweep into white, hold the white to the surface and pull the last stroke through. What in fact you have done after painting the first two petals is increase the white on the petals numbered 3, 5 and 7.

For the skirt, working one petal at a time, push out the edge in Snow White. Pull down with Yellow Light. The dot stamens in the centre are Antique Gold Deep and Snow White.

Oxblood chrysanthemum Fan-out the centre using Oxblood, Antique Gold Deep and Ebony Black. Wash the brush and follow the same method as for the yellow frilly chrysanthemum, this time loading the brush in Oxblood, sweeping through Antique Gold Deep, then sweeping in Snow White. Sweep in Snow White only for every second stroke thereafter. Use the same colours for the skirt, but after sweeping through the Antique Gold Deep *sideload* the

Ball flower

Yellow daisy

Yellow frilly chrysanthemum

Snow White rather than sweeping through it. Hold the white to the outside and pull the strokes into the centre bottom of the flower. The stamens are very fine lines of Snow White. The little turnbacks on the centre front petals are painted in Snow White.

Tulips These are both painted in the same manner. The yellow tulip uses Yellow Light + Snow White, while the oxblood tulip uses Oxblood, Antique Gold Deep and Snow White. With both tulips hold the white in the same direction, that is, to the left. Turn the white to the surface for the centre stroke and blend slightly. The oxblood tulip has two extra small petals which are placed first. These haven't any white on them—they are just Oxblood and Antique Gold Deep.

At this stage, review your work and add any necessary filler comma strokes with the dark leaf mix and a little Antique Gold Deep swept in.

Little daisies These are painted with Antique Gold Deep and Snow White; their centres are Oxblood and Antique Gold Deep. Do not try to make the little petals even.

Vines and tendrils Paint in the dark leaf mix (Black Forest Green + Ebony Black).

Side pattern
Repeat 6 times around box.

Ribbon Thin down Snow White and place in the ribbon, flipping the brush every few centimetres to make the ribbon twist.

Leaves and daisies Use the same mixes as for the lid.

I decided not to antique this piece because the colours pleased me as they were—lovely and crisp—but if you decide to antique follow the instructions on page 9.

Varnish with the appropriate varnish.

Memory box
Pattern on page 72

Wash in the extra little filler leaves with watery teal green. All you are doing is adding colour behind the roses

Palette (Jo Sonja colours)
Burgundy
Moss Green
Teal Green
French Blue
Titanium White
Clear Glazing Medium

This little box has been washed with French Blue + Clear Glazing Medium. Test the colour on the bottom of the box first, and if too opaque add more medium. Wipe off any excess with an old rag, in the direction of the grain. Lightly trace on the centre oval pattern and using a heavier mix of French Blue + Clear Glazing Medium (that is, more paint less medium), slip-slap this into the oval. Aim for a casual broken-up effect. Sand the box, removing some of the paint from the edges. Recoat with Clear Glazing Medium.

Leaves When the box is dry freehand in the leaves rather than tracing them on. Refer to the colour work-up. The leaves are painted in Teal Green. Remember they are only small so keep up on the tip of the brush. For the soft leaves wash in some comma strokes among the solid ones. When dry, trace on the rest of the pattern.

Roses Please refer to the colour work-up on page 14, but remember the roses there are larger than those actually painted on the box. Check the pattern to see the correct size. Mix Moss Green + Burgundy to get a dark pink. To half of this add some white to make a soft pink. With the dark mix paint a small circle, sweep through the paler mix, and sideload the white. Hold the white to the outside at all times. Start at the back and push out the back centre petals. Sideload into more white, remembering to keep up on the tip, and place in the two petals on the body of the rose, then the two side petals, and lastly the one at the bottom of the rose.

Dot daisies White with a Burgundy centre.

Wash leaves and filler leaves Thin down the Teal Green and wash in small commas wherever you feel there is a gap. Add long stems for the tiny daisy buds, which are in Titanium White. Thin down the Titanium White with water and paint a daisy outline in any gaps.

Writing and line work The writing is also painted in the thinned paint. The verse is:

ACT JUSTLY,
LOVE TENDERLY,
WALK HUMBLY.

Paint the line on the lid drop and the top of the bottom of the box.

Varnish with your preferred method. I have used four coats of Clear Glazing Medium.

Waiting stool

Pattern on pages 68–69

Palette (Jo Sonja colours)
Smoked Pearl
Red Earth
Raw Umber
Burnt Umber
Warm White
Yellow Oxide
Pine Green
Storm Blue
Clear Glazing Medium
masking tape

I thought I would try some soft and easy washes on this stool. I was undecided about the pattern—it's not in the usually heavier style of most folk art. Remember to keep everything nice and soft. Start off with just a hint of colour, as you can always add more.

Mix Smoked Pearl and Clear Glazing Medium and 'pickle' the wood with this mix. All this means is paint it on and wipe it off with a soft cloth. You will have a soft creamy colour with the wood grain still plainly visible. (Craftwood is unsuitable for this project.) Sand the surface lightly.

Measure off the lattice border and run masking tape down each side to keep the inside edges neat. Thin Raw Umber and paint the lattice. Keep it free and loose. You can use a liner or a round brush. Measure 2 cm (¾") in from the edge on the long side of the seat and wash this area with Red Earth. Paint a Raw Umber line on the inside edge. Continue the Red Earth wash around the other cut edges. Dry, and apply the pattern using the chalk method.

The scene Outline the doorway and canopy with Burnt Umber, remembering to keep the paint thin. Using Warm White, wash in either side of the doorway, working in a little Burnt Umber for shadow as you near the canopy.

Moisten the interior of the doorway with water. Start at the top left corner and, working quickly, slip-slap Burnt Umber into the corner, fading it out as you near the bottom left-hand corner. You may like to work a little Yellow Oxide and/or Warm White into the Burnt Umber as you move down. Don't labour over this or you may overwork the area and it will become a uniform colour. The canopy is Red Earth with a little Burnt Umber worked in. Separate the tiles with Burnt Umber, and outline everything with a broken watery line of Burnt Umber. Mix Burnt Umber + Warm White and paint the stone surround around the door and the step. Shade with Burnt Umber near the top, and at the side of the step. Place in thin lines of Burnt Umber to represent the bricks. Paint around the edge of the window and shade down the side and the ledge, again with Burnt Umber. Use a little Storm Blue mixed with a tiny dot of Burnt Umber to wash in the window pane.

Mix Pine Green + Burnt Umber and paint the stem and the leaves on the climbing rose. The roses are tiny comma strokes of Red Earth sideloaded in Warm White. The potplant is outlined in Burnt Umber and washed in with Red Earth. There is a little shading with Burnt Umber on the sides. The flowers are Titanium White, with the leaves and stems the same mix as the rose.

The chicks are blocked in with Yellow Oxide and their wings highlighted with Titanium White. Eyes and feet are Carbon Black. The grains of seed are tiny dots of Burnt Umber. The bowl is outlined in a mix of Carbon Black + Titanium White. Highlight with the same mix but add more white. The puppy is casually outlined in Burnt Umber then filled in with a wash of Titanium White. His patches are Burnt Umber.

Geraniums Outline the leaves with a mix of Pine Green + Burnt Umber. Thin the paint to facilitate the flow and break the line rather than making it solid. Use this mix, thinned, to colour in the leaves. Any areas that need shading should be gone over again. The flowers are washed in with Red Earth. Place in all the petals, then go over some of them again to add depth.

Finish with three coats of varnish.

Picture frame
Pattern on page 73

Palette (Jo Sonja colours)
Titanium White
Yellow Oxide
Storm Blue
Burgundy
Moss Green
Teal Green

Mix Teal Green and Titanium White to make a soft green for the basecoat. You will only need a little teal and lots of white.

Seal the surface first with one coat of Jo Sonja All-Purpose Sealer. Sand lightly and apply the basecoat. You will probably need three coats, sanding between. Apply the pattern using the chalk method.

Ribbon Mix Storm Blue with a little Titanium White and reduce the consistency of the paint by adding water. Sideload in fresh Titanium White and softly blend on the palette, in the same place, two or three times. The brush should be flat with white on one side, Storm Blue mix on the other and a soft blend of the two in between. Hold the brush on the knife edge to start the ribbon, then lay it down with the white turned to the outside, pick it up and now turn the white to the inside. Complete the bow using this method.

Leaves and stems Three shades of paint are used:
 Teal Green
 Teal + Titanium White
 Watery Teal Green

Choose the leaves you would like to paint in each of the three shades. I freehanded mine in at random starting with the darker colour.

Blossoms Refer to the work-up. The colour is a soft pink made by mixing Burgundy and Moss Green (dark mix), and adding Titanium White to make a soft pale pink. Remember acrylic paints dry about two shades darker, so take this into account when mixing.

Sideload in Titanium White and, working one petal at a time, lay down the white. Wipe the brush, flatten in the lighter pink and pull down the white. Repeat this for all the petals. The centres are Yellow Oxide stippled in with a highlight of Titanium White. The stamens are Titanium White and the pollen dots are the dark pink mix. The buds are small S strokes painted in the dark pink mix. They have Teal Green calyxes.

Forget-me-nots Storm Blue + Titanium White with Yellow Oxide centres.

Randomly pull out little thin sprigs of Teal Green around the outside of the design. They can have tiny Titanium White dots on the ends if you like. Dry and varnish in your preferred method.

Pansy box
Pattern on page 72

Palette (Jo Sonja colours)
Indian Red Oxide
Storm Blue
Smoked Pearl
Teal Green
Green Oxide
Rich Gold
Cadmium Yellow Mid
Diox Purple
Titanium White
Ultramarine Blue
Burgundy
Clear Glazing Medium
Retarder and Antiquing Medium

Trace the perimeter of the design onto the box using the chalk method. Don't press too hard or you will dent the soft pine surface. Using a large flat brush wash in the outside areas of the design with Indian Red Oxide. Add plenty of water to help the paint flow quickly. Don't get too dark. Dry.

Now, using Smoked Pearl and Clear Glazing Medium, lightly coat the inside area of the design where the pansies will sit. While this is still wet, pick up a tiny amount of Retarder plus Indian Red Oxide and work this onto the area beneath the pansies. If you find this drying too quickly pick up a little more Retarder. Now take a little Storm Blue and work this in also. Try and use a slip-slap action as this helps stop the two colours from blending together. Aim for a soft muted effect (see colour work-up). Dry. Apply one coat of Clear Glazing Medium, and sand lightly. Trace on the rest of the pattern.

Scrolls Thin Rich Gold with a little water.

Leaves and calyx These are painted in Teal Green with a sideload of Green Oxide and are painted in comma stroke fashion. The comma strokes are straight Teal Green.

Pansies Revise the fan-out method on page 11 to familiarise yourself with this technique. The pansies are all painted in the same way but use different colours. Refer to the pattern for the corresponding numbers.
1. Storm Blue + Indian Red Oxide
2. Ultramarine Blue + Burgundy
3. Diox Purple

The order of painting is as follows:
1. Paint the very back petals.
2. Paint the next two back petals.
3. Using the fan-out method, paint the centre of the front petal.
4. Finish the front petal, gently pulling the colour into the edge of the fanned-out paint.

Pansy No. 1 Sideload into Titanium White and, working only one of the back petals at a time, lay down the white. Wipe the brush and sweep through mix 1. Pull the white down to the centre of the pansy, taking note of the direction of the petal. Half of the back petal is under the middle pansy, so don't carry the sideload of white into that area or you will end up with ridges when you come to paint the top pansy. Apply a very small amount of Antiquing and Retarder Medium to the front petal. A slight sheen on the surface is all that is needed. If it is very wet and shiny you have too much and will need to absorb some with a paper towel.

Load the brush in Cadmium Yellow Mid and place a spot of Carbon Black near the ferrule. Fan out the centre, keeping the black confined to the area in the centre. Wash the brush to get rid of the black, sideload in Titanium White and finish the petal as before. Don't pull the mix up into the fanned-out area, rather keep it to the edges.

Complete the other two pansies in the same way except for the fanned-out centres. Use the corresponding mixes given below.

Pansy No. 2 Load the brush in Diox Purple and place a Cadmium Yellow Mid dot near the ferrule.

Pansy No. 3 Load the brush in Cadmium Yellow Mid and place a Carbon Black dot near the ferrule.

The comma strokes at the centre of the petals are Cadmium Yellow Mid for pansies nos 1 and 3, and Diox Purple for pansy no. 2. All have Titanium White dots. I have pulled out tiny feathery lines from the centre dot in the corresponding colour.

The pansy on the front of the box is the same as pansy no. 2.

Varnish using your preferred varnish, or try mixing 1 part Jo Sonja Clear Glazing Medium to 1 part Jo Sonja Satin Finishing Varnish and using this to finish your piece. It gives a beautiful soft finish, but you need to apply three or four coats.

Photo album
Pattern on pages 74–75

Palette (DecoArt colours)
Moon Yellow
Snow White
Antique Green
Ebony Black
Jo Sonja Clear Glazing Medium (optional)

You also need a découpage picture ready to apply to the album. Check the pattern for the size you need and see page 13 for instructions on how to prepare the picture. Trim the prepared picture to the correct sized oval to fit the flower surround.

Centre the picture onto the album and *lightly* chalk in the edges. Remove the picture, and on the reverse side, thinly spread on some Jo Sonja All-Purpose Sealer, working with the picture laid face down on plastic, as described on page 13. You will need disposable gloves to do this. Position the picture on the album and, working from the centre, gently push any bubbles or wrinkles out. The picture will stretch quite easily so be careful (or you may end up with a very odd looking person on the front of your album!). If any corners or edges lift, stick them back down and apply a little pressure until they adhere. Try not to get sealer on the wood as it will be noticeable when the colour is applied.

Notice the Antique Gold has been used to suggest folds in the morning glory flowers

If you find that you have spilled some outside the edges of the picture, take a damp cloth and wipe it off as soon as possible.

Let dry thoroughly. Do not use a hair dryer as this may cause the picture to bubble.

Wash Thin down the Moon Yellow with sufficient water to make a wash. Starting at the sides of the découpaged picture, pull the wash to the outside edges, covering the entire exposed wooden surface. Dry and sand lightly. I gave my piece one coat of Jo Sonja Clear Glazing Medium at this stage. This helps if you need to remove a mistake because the wood is not so porous. Apply the pattern.

Leaves Mix Antique Green + Ebony Black to get a good dark green. Lay Antique Green across the back section of the leaf, and using the dark mix pull the lighter green down. For the front or turned up part, mix Antique Green with a little Snow White and push this out around the edge of that section. Use Antique Green to pull the lighter colour down. Try and give the leaves a lot of movement, and remember to keep an eye on the direction of your strokes.

Stems Use the liner brush and thinned dark mix to paint all the stems in, keeping them nice and thin. Add some wash leaves at this stage if you would like.

Morning glory These flowers are very frilly, so try and follow the pattern when you lay down the Snow White. Work half the flower at a time. Wipe the brush and sweep through Snow White, now pull the thick white edge down. At the back of the petals sweep through a little Antique Gold Deep after sweeping through the white. This adds depth and the appearance of folds to the petals. See colour work-up.

Buds Little S strokes of Snow White sideloaded in Antique Gold Deep.

Calyx These are the same dark mix as the leaves. Sweep through a little Antique Gold, and hold this to the surface for the middle stroke.

Let the work dry, and antique using Burnt Umber oil paint. This will considerably tone the wood. I suggest you try the colour inside the back cover first. Leave the work to dry for a few days after antiquing, and finally finish off with some good quality paste wax rubbed in with a pad of steel wool (000 or 0000).

Sally's cupboard
Pattern on pages 76–77

My lovely friend Sally Luck helped me prepare this piece. It's great to have friends that don't mind the dirty work—thanks, Sal.

Palette (DecoArt colours)
Flesh Tone
Enid's Collection
Oxblood
Brilliant Red
Antique Green
Antique Gold Deep
Blue Green
Ebony Black
Snow White
Sealer

Give the raw wood surface one coat of DecoArt Sealer. Sand lightly when dry and apply Fleshtone with a large flat brush. You will probably need several coats to give an opaque finish. Keep going! Sand lightly when dry. Position the pattern on the piece, making sure that it's centred both vertically and horizontally. Trace the pot and pole.

Pole Using masking tape, mask down either side of the pole. Block in this area with Antique Gold Deep. Make certain it's opaque. Mix Brilliant Red and Antique Green to make a warm Burnt Sienna. Moisten one side of the pole with water and wash a fairly transparent line of the Burnt Sienna mix down the length of the pole. Try and bring the colour towards the middle so the pole will appear rounded, but keep an area in the centre free of the Burnt Sienna mix. You are only working in a small area so it's a little tricky. Repeat for the other side when this side has dried.

Pot Give the surface one coat of Antique Gold Deep. You should be able to still see the lines of the pattern. Work on the bottom section of the pot first. Recoat this area only and let dry. Apply another coat, then, using the same Burnt Sienna mix from the pole, start at the edge and walk the colour across to the other side. You will find that you will only need a small amount of paint. When dry repeat for the other side (see colour work-up).

You will notice I have left the centre of the pot free of Burnt Sienna. Recoat the rim area and shade that in the same way. I have also shaded under the rim on the body of the pot. Make sure this area is dry or you will pick up what you have already painted. Using the same Burnt Sienna Mix recoat the back section of the pot. This area was Antique Gold Deep, and you will need a few coats.

Using Snow White dry brush some highlights down the centre of the pot and rim. They should be very soft. Carefully tidy up any edges. Use Fleshtone to restore the basecoat if needed.

Topiary top Reapply the pattern to your piece; using the chalk method roughly mark in the outside perimeter of the design. Mix Antique Green with Ebony Black and thin with water to get a transparent look. Remember to absorb some of the watery paint on paper towel to avoid 'puddling'. With the chalk pattern as a guide, paint foliage using commas and S strokes inside the area, pulling all the stems towards the top of the pole. You are giving depth and interest to the area behind the pattern. A lot of this work will be covered, but the finished design would look naked without it. You may like to pull a few wispy leaves and tendrils outside the pattern area. When dry apply the pattern.

Leaves Mix Antique Green + Ebony Black to get a dark green. Base in the leaves solidly. You will need at least two coats.
Tulip leaves Give one coat and let that dry. Sideload for the second coat in Antique Gold Deep. Pull all the stems down toward the top of the pole, even though they don't appear on the pattern.

The techniques for the roses and chrysanthemums are covered under the step by step instructions for each flower on pages 14 and 16. Here I give the colours used for each flower in this design.

Chrysanthemums Fan-out the centre using Oxblood, Antique Gold Deep and Ebony Black. Wash the brush, load in Oxblood, sweep through Antique Gold Deep, then Snow White, and complete the flower. The same colours are used for the skirts. The centres are different, the top flower with the frilly skirt having tiny Antique Gold Deep dots, while the bottom one has very fine stamens of Snow White.

Roses The roses also have fan-out centres using a mix of Brilliant Red + Antique Green to make the lovely Burnt Sienna used earlier. The colours here are Burnt Sienna mix, Antique Gold Deep and Ebony Black. The petals on the body of the rose have a Snow White pull-in edge. The white has been pulled down with the brush loaded in Burnt Sienna mix then swept through Antique Gold Deep, holding the gold to the surface. The skirt uses these same colours. The centres on both roses have Antique Gold Deep and Snow White tiny dots.

Daisies Push out the edge of the petal with Snow White. Wipe the brush, sweep through Blue Green, and use this to pull the white down. Repeat this for all the petals. The centres are Antique Gold Deep, with a shade of Oxblood dabbled on one side, and a highlight of Snow White on the other.

Tulips The top tulip uses Oxblood, Antique Gold Deep and Snow White. The bottom tulip, near the pole, uses Yellow Light, Antique Gold Deep and Snow White. These instructions are for the top tulip; adjust the colours as necessary for the bottom one.

Load the brush in Oxblood, sweep through Antique Gold Deep and sideload the Snow White. With the sideloaded white held to the right, paint an S stroke. Repeat for the other side, still keeping the white to the right. Sideload into more white, and with the white again to the right place in the centre petal. (See colour work-up.) Sideload white again, but this time hold the white to the surface and pull the stroke through.

The tiny dots are Snow White with Antique Gold Deep centres.

Ribbon Using the same Burnt Sienna mix, sideload in Snow White and blend softly on the palette. Hold the white to the top and following the pattern, complete the bow. Touch into a drop of water if you feel the paint is too dry.

Stand back from your work and assess the piece as a whole. Add any filler strokes or wash foliage as needed. Don't overdo it.

When dry antique lightly with Burnt Umber and varnish with the appropriate varnish.

Michael's tray
Pattern on pages 78–79

Our eldest son loves the scene on this tray—hence the name. This is actually a wall tray so when not in use it can hang on the kitchen wall for everyone to admire.

Palette (Jo Sonja colours)
Paynes Grey
Storm Blue
Titanium White
Yellow Oxide
Brown Earth
Moss Green
Red Earth
Antique Green
Ultramarine
Raw Sienna
Napthol Red Light
Antique Gold
Carbon Black
All-Purpose Sealer
flat brushes in sizes 2 and 6 (optional)

The scene on this piece is more easily painted with flat brushes. You really don't use any special techniques—it's just easier to cover the areas with a flat brush. If you would rather use a round brush, that's fine too.

Seal the entire surface with one coat of Jo Sonja All-Purpose Sealer. Sand lightly. Now, mix the sealer 1:1 into some Yellow Oxide and paint the outside rim and drop. Mix more sealer 1:1 with Antique Green and basecoat the base of the tray and the small inside drop. Make sure you have a smooth finish with no ridges or wrinkles. Trace the scene onto the surface (don't forget to centre it) using the chalk method. Omit the boats, houses and trees as you will be painting over them.

Sea Moisten the area with water, and using Storm Blue cover the area as quickly as you can. Now pick up a little Yellow Oxide and work that into the sea near the land. On the corner of the brush pick up a little Titanium White and place in the waves. Remember they are very small. Try and be casual and don't labour over this as it should appear fairly loose.

Sky Moisten the area with water. Pick up Storm Blue and Titanium White on the corner of your brush and work this across the sky. Make it lighter behind the hills. While still wet pick up more white and place in the clouds. A little Yellow Oxide worked in between the clouds is a nice touch.

Hills There are four hills. The large hill in the middle is painted with Paynes Grey. You can play a little here but keep it loose. This mountain range has snow on it so pick up a little white and work that in. As you move down towards the beach pick up a little Brown Earth, but don't wash your brush in between. Hill no. 2 is Brown Earth with Moss Green brush-mixed on your piece. Hills no. 3 and 4 are this mix also, with a little Titanium White. The sandy beach area is a fine line of Brown Earth.

Trees Use the corner of the large flat brush, or a small flat brush, and just dab in various mixes of Brown Earth and Moss Green. The trunks are Brown Earth. Trace on the rest of the pattern.

Houses Mix Paynes Grey and Titanium White together. You will only need a very small amount. Using the size 2 flat brush, place them in. Choose whichever houses and buildings you like. The roofs and shade side of the buildings are a darker mix of the wall colour. The other colour mix is Titanium White plus a little Yellow Oxide. The church is straight white. The windows are Paynes Grey. Use your liner brush and thin the paint down. The flagpole is Brown Earth and the flag is Titanium White.

Ships The one at the back (you can hardly see it) is based in with a dark grey mix of Carbon Black plus Titanium White. Add highlights of Yellow Oxide. The funnel and rigging are Brown Earth. The smoke is Titanium White.

The front ship is based in with Red Earth. The stern is outlined in Yellow Oxide. The rigging is Brown Earth and the sails Titanium White.

Scroll border Trace on the scroll border and paint in the scrolls with Yellow Oxide sideloaded in Titanium White. The separate dark commas are Brown Earth. When dry, trace on the rest of the pattern. The pattern on my tray is not symmetrical; if this worries you flip it over and trace it through that way for the other end. I sometimes like my work to have an element of surprise rather than being predictable.

Leaves Base the leaves in with a mixture of Ultramarine Blue, Raw Sienna and a touch of Carbon Black. You will need two coats, so try and base them in smoothly—no ridges. The knife strokes on the leaves can be left until the end. They are painted in the dark leaf mix, but sweep through Raw Sienna after loading. Any filler comma strokes you may wish to add can be left to the end. They are painted in the same colours as the knife strokes. Retrace the flowers if you feel you need to.

Roses The roses all have fan-out centres. For the red roses use Napthol Red Light, Antique Gold and Carbon Black. For the yellow roses use Raw Sienna, Antique Gold and Carbon Black.
The red rose Mix Napthol Red Light + Raw Sienna to achieve a warm red. Push out the petals with Titanium White and pull the white down with the brush loaded in this mix and swept through Antique Gold. Remember to work one petal at a time, and look at the direction of your strokes. Add fine white stamens in the centre.
The yellow rose Load the brush in Raw Sienna, sweep through Antique Gold and use this to pull the white down. The stamens are white also.

Daisies Push out the edge of the petals in Titanium White. Mix Ultramarine Blue with a little Carbon Black and use this mix to pull the white down. The centres are Antique Gold with a little shade colour of Napthol Red Light + Raw Sienna dabbled on one side and Titanium White on the other.

When dry antique with burnt umber oil paint using the antiquing method on page 9. Varnish with the appropriate varnish for use over oil antiquing, preferably satin.

See page 58 for work-up

Colour work-up for Michael's tray (page 56). Outline the houses and buildings in Paynes Grey. See page 14 for flower work-up.

PATTERNS
Treasure chest
Page 18

You can make up any insects or bugs that you like

The plate
Page 24

Poppy plaque
Page 21

match crosses to join

join here

match crosses to join

65

Lace box
Page 31

Repeat pattern

67

Waiting stool
Page 41

Flower basket box
Page 35

match crosses to join

Side pattern—
repeat 6 times

Memory box
Page 38

Pansy box
Page 47

Picture frame
Page 44

Photo album
Page 50

Sally's cupboard
Page 52

Lightly chalk the outline of the pattern onto your piece. Wash foliage in behind, pulling all the stems into the centre of the design

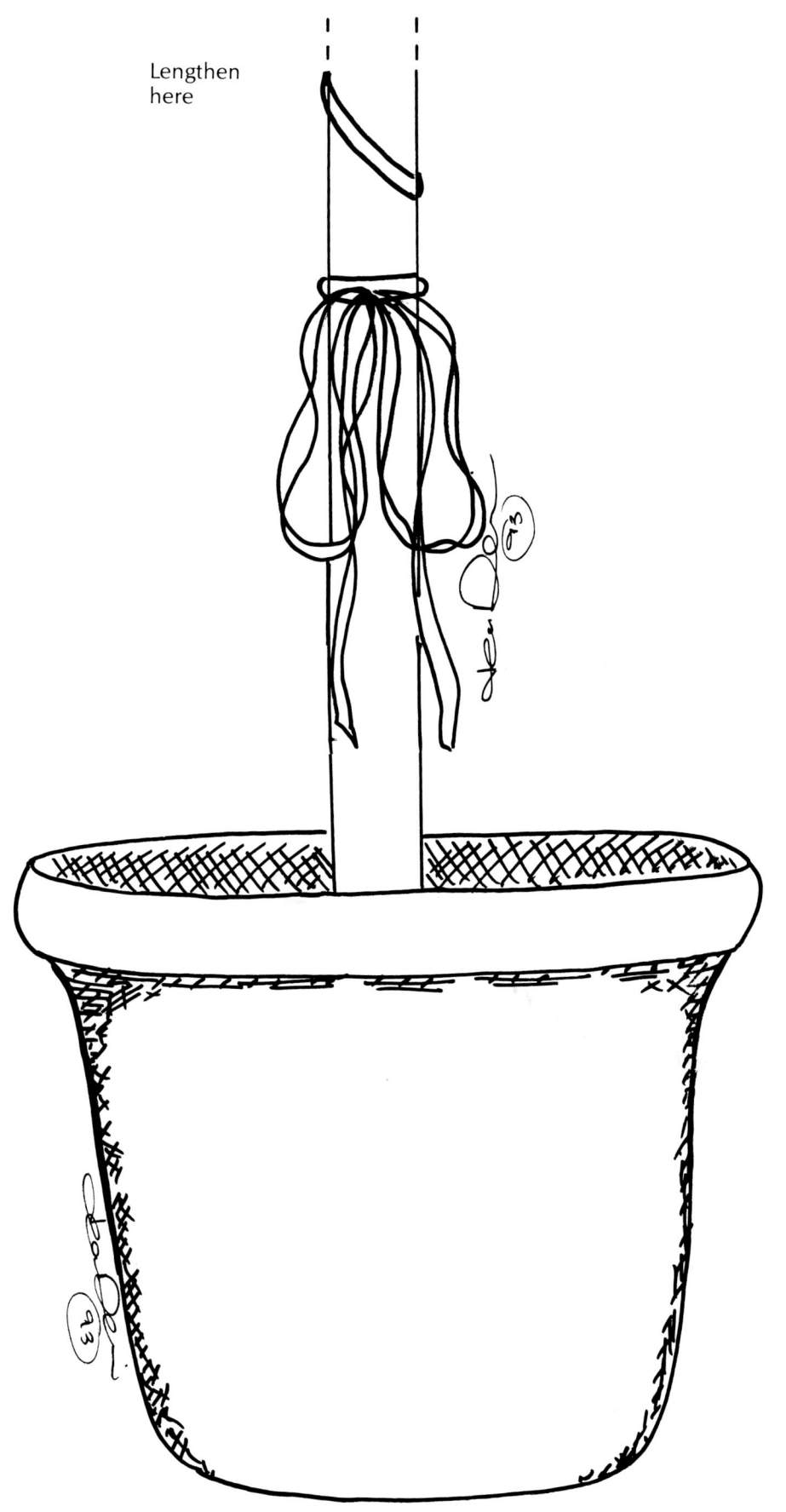

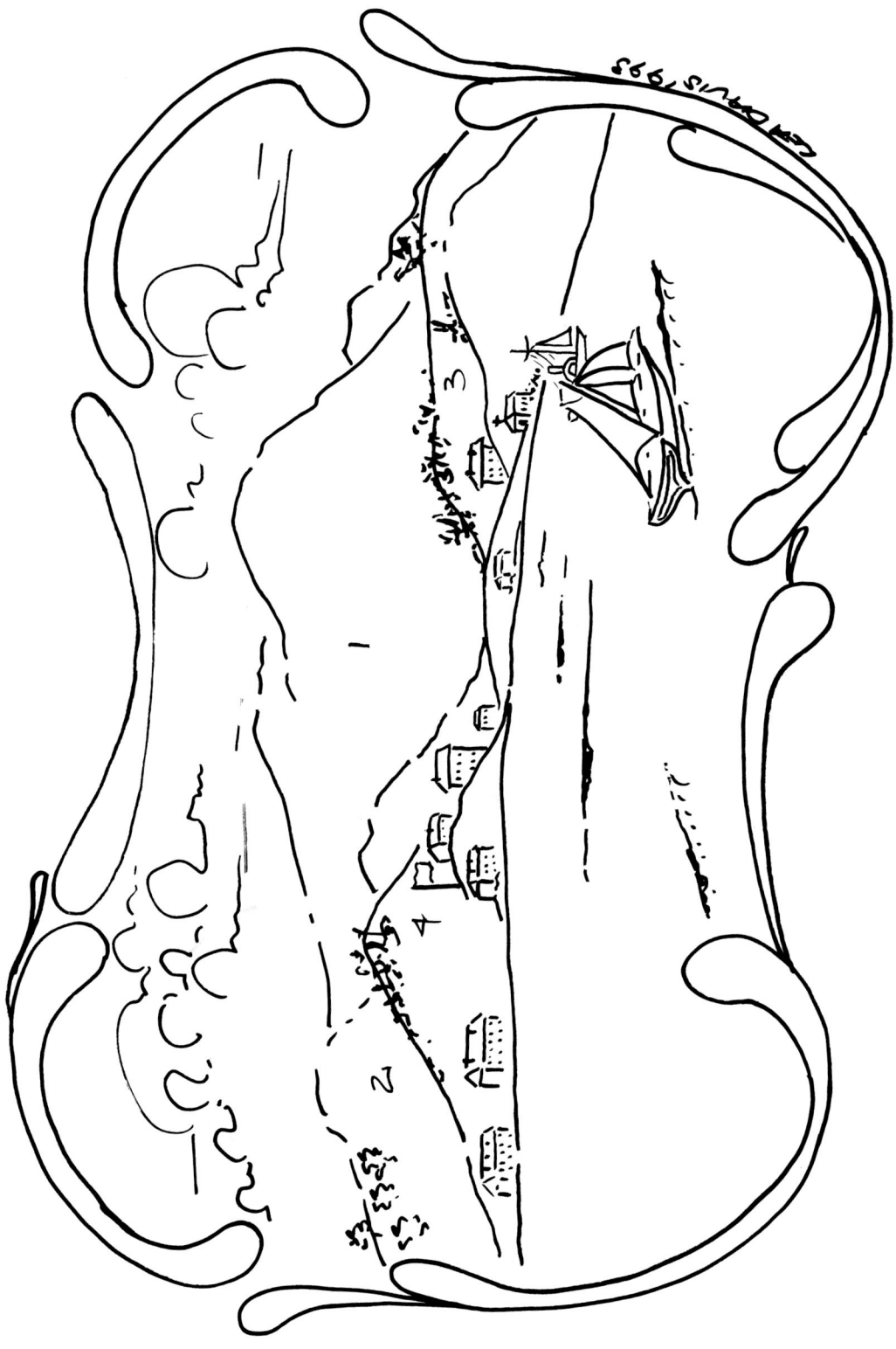

Michael's tray
Page 56

Suppliers

Victorian Academy of Decorative Art
369 Camberwell Rd
Camberwell Vic. 3124
(03) 882-7082
Fax: (03) 882-9128
Please contact these experienced folk artists for any help you may need. The following pieces (plus lots more) are available from there:
  Primo Palettes
  Treasure Chest (page 18)
  Picture Frame (page 44)
  Michael's Tray (page 56)
  Poppy Plaque (page 21)
  Waiting Stool (page 41)
also Black Etch Printer

Boyle Industries (wholesale only)
Factory 4
14 Apollo Court
Blackburn Vic. 3130
(03) 894-2233
Fax: (03) 894-2382
  Plate (page 24)
  Lace Box (page 31)
  Pansy Box (page 47)
  Memory Box (page 38)
Ask your craft store to contact these friendly and courteous people for really cheap wooden items. They also have an extensive range of craft items.

Timber Turn (wholesale only)
1 Shepley Avenue
Panorama SA 5041
(08) 277-5056
Fax: (08) 277-5540
  Photo Album (page 50)
  35 cm Flower Basket Box (page 35)
Robert and Virginia Brown have the most wonderful array of wooden items imaginable. Your local craft store would be able to order them for you. Please enquire.

Index

Antiquing, 9

Basecoating, 8
Basic loading, 10
Brushes, 8

Chalk method, 8

Dry brushing, 12

Fan-out centre, 11
Flat brush, 57

Graphite paper, 8
Gum turpentine, 9

Knife edge, 10
Knife stroke, 10

Linseed oil, 9

Natural turpentine, 9

Oil paint, 9

Palette, 8
Paper towel, 8
Paste wax, 51

Patina oil, 9
Pickle, 41
Pull-in, 11

Retarder, 35

Sandpaper, 8
Sealing, 9
Sideload, 11
Steel wool, 51
Stipple, 11
Stylus, 8
Sweep, 11

Tipping, 11
'To the surface', 10
'To the ceiling', 10
Transferring a pattern
  chalk, 8
  transfer paper, 8
Turnback, 14, 23

Varnish, 9

Wash, 10
Wax, 51